Stitch Kitsch

Jennifer Heynen

44 Happy Sewing Projects from Home Decor to Accessories

stashBOOKS
an imprint of C&T Publishing

Text copyright © 2015 by Jennifer Heynen

Photography and artwork copyright © 2015 by C&T Publishing, Inc.

Publisher: Amy Marson

Creative Director: Gailen Runge

Art Director/Cover Designer: Kristy Zacharias

Editor: Liz Aneloski

Technical Editors: Susan Hendrickson and Debbie Rodgers

Book Designer: Casey Dukes

Production Coordinator: Jenny Davis and Freesia Pearson Blizard

Production Editor: Joanna Burgarino

Illustrator: Rue Flaherty

Photo Assistant: Mary Peyton Peppo

Style photography by Nissa Brehmer and instructional photography by Diane Pedersen, unless otherwise noted

Published by Stash Books, an imprint of C&T Publishing, Inc., P.O. Box 1456, Lafayette, CA 94549

Library of Congress Cataloging-in-Publication Data

Heynen, Jennifer.

 Stitch kitsch : 44 happy sewing projects from home decor to accessories / Jennifer Heynen.

  pages cm

 ISBN 978-1-61745-055-6 (soft cover)

 1. Sewing. 2. House furnishings. I. Title.

 TT387.H49 2015

 746.44--dc23

              2015008952

Printed in China

10 9 8 7 6 5 4 3 2 1

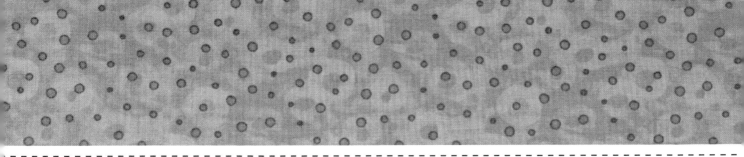

Acknowledgments

This book is dedicated to my husband, Nik, and my boys, Fletcher and Birkley.

I would like to thank:

Nik, Fletcher, and Birkley for listening to me go on and on about sewing projects and giving me feedback on ideas when you were probably thinking you'd like to be doing just about anything else. Thanks for showing me you care.

My parents, because now that I have older children, I realize how brave you were to let your child wear wild clothes to school and then send her off to college to get a degree in ceramics.

The rest of my family, Chris, Hazel, Hendrix, Linda, and Jim.

Jason at In the Beginning Fabrics for *always* considering my crazy ideas and trusting that some of them might work out. Thank you for teaching me so much about the fabric world. And to Leah, Paula, Wendy, and everyone else at ITB for working so hard and always making me look good.

Gailen, Roxane, Liz, Susan, and everyone at C&T for having the excitement and giving me the support I needed to write this book. I am honored to have a C&T book.

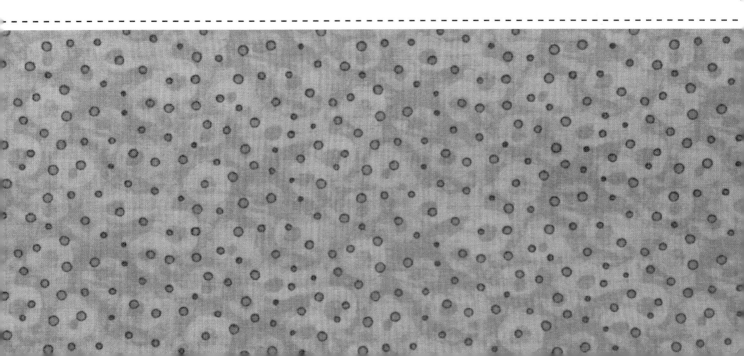

Contents

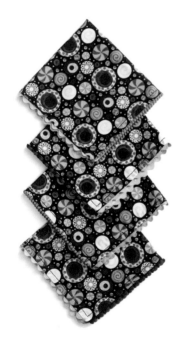

Foreword

I believe that my early years of sewing and designing, making my own clothes in high school, my ceramics business, and my parents support all were part of my journey to get to where I am now and what I do. Don't be afraid to try everything: new techniques, new mediums, things you think would never interest you. Something from all of these experiences always sticks with you and takes you on your journey. I hope some of my projects teach you something new and add to your journey as a sewist.

Introduction

When I set out to write this book, I had three goals in mind: to give you more confidence as a sewist, to inspire you, and to provide you with new embellishing ideas. None of us has tons of time to sew, including myself. However, when I do have time, I want to make something unique and special as well as have fun.

How many times have you completed a project and not been happy with the results? You could have sewn that stitch a little neater, or the zipper should have been turned around. We all sew because we like the process. The process relaxes some, energizes others, gives an escape, to name a few. If sewing is about the journey, which I believe it is, I say let's make it even more fun. Let's let go and not worry if our stitches are straight, if our colors are matched perfectly, or if our seams are aligned. All of those skills come with time and practice. If we have fun, that's what matters. It's the journey, not the destination.

Or, maybe you're the opposite kind of sewist, always neat and tidy with stitches and really would love to be able to loosen up with your stitching. These projects are a great start to play and try some free-motion embroidery or some fun embellishments that haven't been your style. Gain confidence.

I also want to *inspire* you. The more techniques and projects you try and the more you practice sewing, the more ideas you will have about what to sew next. I find myself constantly full of ideas. This book will show you how to take a project and change a thing or two and end up with something entirely different. Hopefully it will give you ideas of your own to take projects even further than what is shown here.

My third goal is to show ways to *embellish*—add variety, texture, and uniqueness to your project. Embellishing doesn't need to mean hours spent sewing little beads onto a bag for trim; it can simply be a row of gathered tulle or a few felt balls. Adding ribbons, trims, or other items to a project will add variety without adding tons of time.

Besides having fun with the process, I believe you can take a pretty basic project and turn it into something even more wonderful with just a few embellishments, trims, or added stitches. This book will help you take that extra little step. The projects in this book give you the basics and then more ideas. The next chapter is about how to use this book as a starting point to try new projects and create unique projects of your own. I hope you have fun!

How This Book Works
Or, how many projects does this book have?

11 PROJECTS

Do you remember the popular book series for kids in the 1980s called Choose Your Own Adventure? *Stitch Kitsch* is a choose-your-own-adventure book for sewists. In this book, you will find 11 projects. These projects range from simple napkins to quilts. Each of these basic projects has step-by-step instructions to guide you from start to finish.

33 VARIATIONS

Now, here comes the fun part. Each of these 11 projects has 3 variations based on the original project. Instructions for changes and adaptations are included, where necessary. Changes might be to add different embellishments, turn a bag into a pillow, or choose a different appliqué design. This is just the beginning of the projects you could make. I hope it opens your eyes and inspires you to continue mixing up colors, designs, embellishments, and more. The sky really is the limit.

You'll find plenty of projects to make as gifts for babies, children, friends, and family. With the embellishing and inspiration to mix and match projects, you'll be able to make a one-of-a-kind gift for anyone on your list. Just imagine a spectacular gift using your grandma's old buttons, your favorite trims, or anything special you've collected.

HUNDREDS OF OPTIONS (A.K.A. EVEN MORE CUSTOMIZING)

All quilts use 6″ blocks, so you can make a quilt any size you want, from a baby blanket all the way to a king-size quilt just by adding blocks.

The bags are simply constructed, so you can change the measurements to make any size you want and still follow the book's instructions. It's the same with the table runners, zipper pouches, pillows…Are you catching the excitement yet? Oh, the possibilities.

I like to embellish everything. Adding another ribbon, button, or flower creates just one more bit of interest to your projects. It does not need to mean hours of sewing on tiny beads or sequins, because most of us don't have time for that. We want quick, fun, and beautiful— and we can have it.

Don't Forget

Let's not forget the journey, a.k.a. letting go and enjoying the process. First of all, embellishing hides a multitude of sins. If you've got a pretty flower on a little zipper pouch, no one is looking at how straight your stitching is—they are looking at the flower. If you sewed that flower on and the seam wasn't a perfect ⅛″, then go over it twice. Heck, go over it again in a different color of thread. It looks like you planned it that way. Embrace that handmade look and push it a little further; you might learn something you didn't know about yourself on the journey.

C'mon, let's get started. This is going to be fun!

USING THE PATTERNS

This book's pattern pullout pages are printed one-sided for your convenience. This means that you can cut out the pullout pieces directly or trace and cut them, if you prefer. The appliqué patterns (page 94) that are printed in the book are meant to be traced onto paper-backed fusible web and then cut.

Things to Collect

If you're like me, you'll use a completely different trim or button on your project than you had originally planned. I like to choose the fabrics, textures, and embellishments as I sew. These are some of the things I like to keep on hand while sewing. It's also useful to have them displayed or organized out in the open where I can see them. In my studio I like to use mason jars, vintage metal and glass bowls, and anything else fun to store my supplies. Try wooden spools for rolling trims.

FABRICS

The fabrics used in the projects are primarily cotton quilting fabrics. A few projects use linen, and this is indicated in the project. Beyond these fabrics are additional fabrics that are used for embellishment.

Ⓐ COTTON AND LINEN

I find myself in awe of how many patterns and colors are available in cotton quilting fabrics. Fabrics that are 100% cotton and cotton blends wash well and are the perfect weight for the projects in the book. By all means, though, try some decorator fabrics for the bags, and fleece or wool for the stuffed bunnies. Remember, this book is all about options.

Ⓑ WOOL

Wool is yet another fun fabric to keep on hand for adding texture. Some small wool companies dye beautiful plain and patterned wools in a huge variety of colors. I use just about any kind of wool I can get my hands on if I like the color. If you're thinking about sewing the Little Ones Stuffed Bunny project, you'll want to look for a tighter woven wool like a suiting wool.

Ⓒ TULLE

I use tulle for adding ruffles and textured layers in flowers. Tulle is inexpensive, so it's easy to keep a variety of colors on hand. Most tulle you find in stores is standard lightweight tulle. Milliners usually carry heavier weights as well.

Ⓓ VELVETEEN

Velveteen is another soft fabric, like velvet. It is a tighter weave and doesn't unravel as easily as velvet. It's usually available in fabric stores in just a few colors, like red, purple, and black. From time to time, I will dye velveteen yardage to keep on hand for embellishing. Be sure to stock up on white or ivory for custom dyeing. Dyeable velveteens and velvets are also sold through specialty retailers for dyeing (see Resources, page 102).

Ⓔ VELVET

Velvet has texture and rich color. It's a very soft fabric. It can be a bit tricky to sew with because it is silky and can unravel at the edges. To keep things less complicated, I use velvet in flowers and other small embellishments. The projects in this book don't require a lot of it, so it's fun to splurge and add it to a project.

Ⓕ FELT

Be sure to keep lots of different colors of felt on hand. I prefer using 100% wool or a wool blend felt. These are softer and cut much nicer than polyester felts and are easy to shop for because they're called wool felt or wool blend felt. I encourage you to try it if you never have; you'll be amazed at how nice it is to sew.

BUTTONS, BEADS, AND MORE

BUTTONS AND BEADS

Buttons and beads are so much fun to collect that I most likely don't need to give you a reason to get some. I pick them up anytime I find something interesting, and they're almost always used in a project. Buttons come in glass, metal, wood, plastic, Bakelite, and more. I love to mix them all.

FELT BALLS

When I think of felt balls, I think of three-dimensional polka dots. They come in a variety of colors and sizes. Sometimes you can find them with stripes, polka dots, or embellishments. They are not beads and therefore do not have holes in them. This is great because they can be sewn on any way you like. Felt balls can also be embroidered for more fun.

POM-POMS AND TASSELS

Pom-poms and tassels go hand in hand with felt balls as embellishments. They take a little more time because often you make them yourself. The good thing is that yarn comes in so many colors that you can have just about any color you want. Try making them with different textures of yarns for an even larger variety.

FOUND OBJECTS

These items are not traditionally used in sewing projects, but I find that they work great for adding an element of interest to a small project.

SMALL VINTAGE ITEMS

Vintage items are always a fun addition to a project. If you're making something like the Holiday Pincushion (page 42), you want to look for something soft that you can push a needle through. If you have a drill, you can make holes in wood pieces for sewing. Some craft suppliers sell button backs that can be glued onto objects to make a button as another option for attaching.

MILLINERY

Millinery items are perfect for sewing onto pincushions and other projects. They are usually small in size and made from foam that can be easily be sewn through. You can find birds, mushrooms, flowers, and other pieces to give you lots of options.

RIBBONS, THREADS, AND TRIMS

Ⓐ TRIMS

There are so many trims on the market that I can't even begin to tell you about all the different kinds. Crochet trims and fringes are a few of my favorites. Grosgrain and silk ribbons come printed and woven in a variety of colors as well, and because they are flat, they are easy to sew on your project. Head to the notions area of your favorite quilt shop to see what you can find.

Ⓑ SARI RIBBON

When I discovered sari ribbon, I fell completely in love. It comes in skeins and is made from discarded Indian saris. The fabric is torn into strips and then sewn together into longer lengths. I like to cut mine into small pieces and use it as fringe. It gives any project a nice shabby chic feel.

Ⓒ RICKRACK

Rickrack is another one of my favorites to keep on hand. I collect all different sizes and colors. It starts small, ¼˝ wide, and goes all the way to 1½˝ wide. Sometimes I shop on Etsy (etsy.com) for vintage rickrack that comes in colors and textures that aren't available anymore.

Ⓓ VELVET RIBBON

The reason I add trims to my work is to add another texture to the fabric. Velvet is one of those trims that automatically adds texture and depth to the project. The colors are very rich, and I find myself using it a lot.

Ⓔ POM-POM TRIM

Pom-pom trim adds instant fun to any project. I love collecting all sorts of sizes and colors. I have even been known to layer my pom-pom trims—I like them that much. Like rickrack, they come in a huge range of sizes and colors.

Ⓕ SIX-STRAND FLOSS

Six-strand floss comes in a huge variety of colors. You can use anywhere from one strand to six strands. Most of the time I used all six strands of floss when embellishing. Six strands are also great for features on stuffed animals.

Ⓖ THREE-STRAND FLOSS

I will admit that I am a lazy stitcher. Some flosses now come in three strands, so six-strand flosses do not need to be separated. I keep a handful of my favorite colors on hand so they are ready for hand stitching. Three-strand floss is nice to use when you want to show your stitches but don't want stitches as heavy as a six-strand floss would give you.

Attaching Embellishments

Machine Top Stitching

You can add a lot of decoration and interest to your project quickly by using your sewing machine. Top stitching can be done just by using the straight stitch and outlining the appliqué in coordinating or black thread. The stitching lines can be stitched over a time or two, depending on how noticeable you want the stitching to be. If you're lucky enough to have a machine with decorative stitches, these can be used for embellishing as well. Most of the appliqué projects in this book are outlined using a buttonhole or straight stitch.

To attach ribbon, sew down each side. It's best to sew from the top to the bottom on each side, instead of turning the fabric around and sewing back to where you started on the other side. Sometimes ribbons have stretch, and stitching in the same direction on both sides will prevent the ribbon from becoming distorted. Stitching close to the edge also helps the ribbon to lie flat.

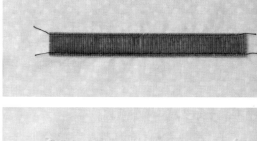

Topstitching rickrack is tricky, because it curves and you can't just sew along the curves unless it's a jumbo rickrack (or you have a lot of time and patience). One option is to sew straight down the middle and leave each side free to curl. Or what I find I like the best is to sew the rickrack in two or three places, depending on the width. This holds the trim in place and adds a bit more detail.

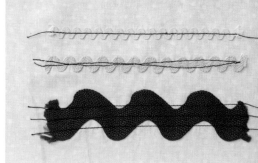

Adding Edge Trim with Machine Stitching

When adding edge trims, instinct would be to place the trim right along the edge of the fabric, but really you should measure ¼˝ in from the edge. This is where the construction stitching will be. Find either the edge of the trim, the center, or where you want the construction stitching to be on the trim, and place it just over the ¼˝ line but within the seam allowance. The trim outside the seam allowance will be visible.

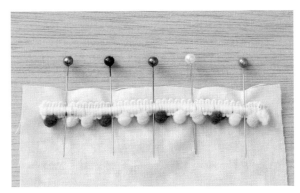

Pin trim.

Finished seam with edge trim

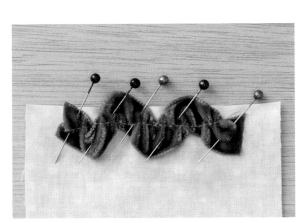

Pin rickrack used as edge trim.

Finished seam with rickrack edge trim

Hand Stitching

Hand stitching is sometimes the easiest way to attach a stack of decorative fabrics to a project. I like to keep a variety of needles on hand. Super sharp, small needles are great for stitching openings closed, whereas a larger soft-sculpture doll needle is great for sewing eyes onto stuffies.

A few of the projects have millinery birds or vintage objects that are typically used for sewing. If these items are soft enough, usually a large needle can be used to poke a hole at the base to stitch through for attaching.

If an item you need to attach has wire legs or stems, a thread that matches the wire can be wrapped around these smaller wires. The matching thread will not show.

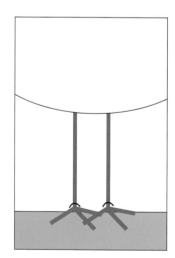

You will find many projects with felt balls throughout the book. Whether it is a half or whole ball, I choose a sewing thread that matches the ball. Just sew through the base of the project and then push the needle through the ball approximately ¼″ from the edge of the ball and out the opposite side to secure. Send the needle back into the base, and repeat this stitch a few times to secure the ball. If the felt ball is cut in half, sew through the project and send the needle through the edge of the base and back out and through the project again. Sew all the way around the base to secure.

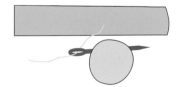

Embroidery

Lots of books are available on embroidery, as well as online tutorials. I won't go into a lot of detail about stitches, but here are some of the basic stitches I used.

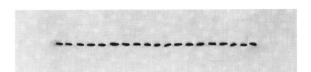

Running stitch

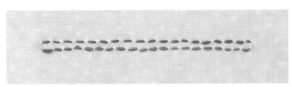

Zipper stitch (two rows of running stitch)

Backstitch

Cross-stitch

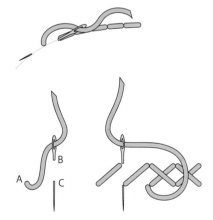

Colorful
TRIMMED NAPKINS

Mix and match these napkins for a dinner party;
you can never have too many. Use theme fabrics
for holidays and birthdays.

Finished size:
16″ × 16″

Note

Make sure all of your trims are washable so that after your dinner party you can throw the napkins in the washing machine. You can always sew a few inches of the trims you plan on using to a scrap piece of quilting cotton. Then throw it in the wash with your next load of laundry and see how they come out. The test trims will most likely have frayed ends when they come out, but your finished napkins won't have any raw trim edges.

CUTTING

Top fabric
- 4 pieces 16½″ × 16½″

Bottom fabric
- 4 pieces 16½″ × 16½″

Trim
- 16 pieces 18″ long

MATERIALS

Makes 4 napkins.

- 1 yard quilting cotton for top fabric
- 1 yard quilting cotton for bottom fabric
- 2¼ yards each of 4 different trims
- All-purpose sewing thread in coordinating colors for assembly
- 3- or 6-strand embroidery floss (if hand stitching) or contrasting all-purpose thread for top stitching

For more information about the materials and techniques used in this project, please see Things to Collect (page 12) and Attaching Embellishments (page 20).

Instructions

Seam allowances are ¼˝.

1. On the right side of the top fabric, pin one of the trims along the edge, making sure that the outer edge of the trim is facing inward. (See Adding Edge Trim with Machine Stitching, page 21.) When you reach the corner, pin the trim so it angles off the napkin. If you're using a pom-pom trim, feel free to cut off one of the pom-poms if it gets in the way of sewing the corner. **Fig. A**

2. Repeat Step 1, pinning the 3 different trims, one on each edge of the napkin. **Fig. B**

3. Place a napkin bottom on the napkin top, right sides together, and pin around all 4 sides. Using a ¼˝ seam allowance and a straight stitch, sew along the edge of the napkin. Leave a 3˝ opening on one side for turning the napkin right side out. **Fig. C**

tip

Use loads of pins when assembling the napkins. Take the pins out one by one as you sew, just as they come to the presser foot, to ensure that the trims don't stretch or slide when sewing.

4. Clip the corners at a 45° angle close to the stitching line, taking care not to clip the stitches. Turn right side out, use a dull pencil to push out the corners, and press. Hand stitch the opening closed. Topstitch around the outside of the napkin ¼˝ from the edge by machine (using a contrasting all-purpose thread) or by hand (using 3- or 6-strand embroidery floss in a contrasting color). **Fig. D**

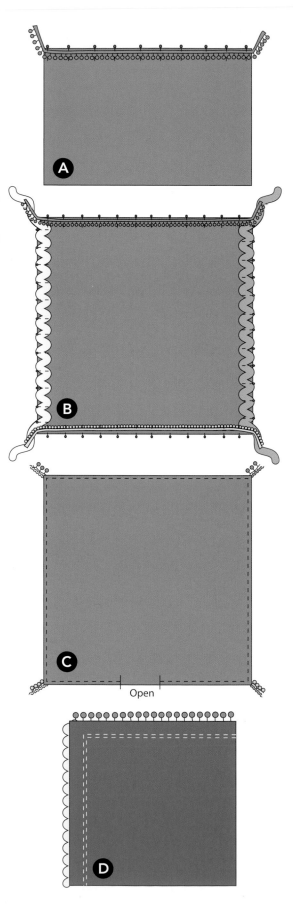

A

B

C

Open

D

Appliqué Napkins

Choose appliqué Patterns 1–4 (pages 94 and 95).
Follow Steps 1–4 in Appliqué Zipper Pouches
(page 32) to add appliqués to one corner of
your napkins.

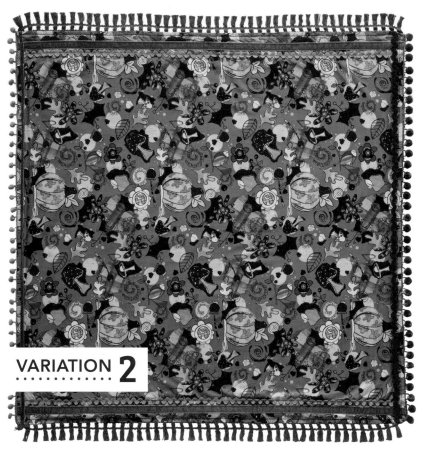

VARIATION 2

Table Square / Tablecloth

Measure your table top to determine the fabric needed to make a table square or tablecloth. Follow the Colorful Trimmed Napkins instructions (page 26).

tip

If your table square/tablecloth needs to be wider than a standard fabric width, avoid a seam down the middle. Use a full-width piece in the center (approximately 42″) and add a narrower strip of fabric to each side to get the width you need.

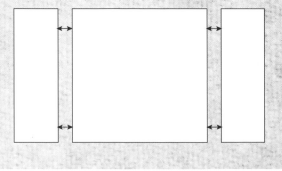

Coasters

For each coaster, cut the 2 fabric squares and a piece of batting 6½˝ × 6½˝. Follow the instructions for Colorful Trimmed Napkins (page 26). At Step 3, place the batting square on top of the coaster fabric stack, pin in place, and sew as instructed.

Appliqué
ZIPPER POUCHES

Decorate these zippered, appliquéd pouches with appliqués and embellishments of your choice. Make them in colors to match each of your handbags. If you have avoided zippers because they seem too hard, give this project a try! They're easier than you think!

Finished size: approximately 5″ × 6″

MATERIALS

Makes 1 pouch.

- ¼ yard or a fat quarter of linen for outer shell

- ¼ yard or a fat quarter of cotton quilting fabric for lining

- 9″ zipper or longer (Zipper is trimmed later to fit.)

- ⅛ yard of 17″-wide paper-backed fusible web

- Assorted fabrics for appliqué (approximately 4–8 fabrics measuring 4″ × 4″)

For more information about the materials and techniques used in this project, please see Things to Collect (page 12) and Attaching Embellishments (page 20).

- 8″ of pom-pom trim, 5 felt balls 1.5cm (¾″), or 24″ of sari ribbon for embellishing

- 3″ of ribbon ¼″–½″ wide for split ring loop

- 1″ split ring

- 3 small buttons ¼″–⅓″ in diameter for flower pouch

- All-purpose sewing thread to match outer shell fabric

- Black all-purpose sewing thread for decorative topstitching

- Nonstick pressing cloth

- *Optional:* ¼ yard of flannel to add padding and weight to the bag

CUTTING

Outer shell

- 2 pieces 5½″ × 6½″

Lining

- 2 pieces 5½″ × 6½″

If using sari ribbon trim

- 5–8 pieces 3″ long

Flannel (*optional*)

- 2 pieces 5½″ × 6½″

Instructions

Seam allowances are ¼˝.

1. Trace Appliqué Pattern 1, 2, 3, or 4 (pages 94 and 95) onto the paper side of the fusible web.

2. Cut out the fusible web approximately ¼˝ outside the drawn line. Place the appliqué fabric right side down on the ironing board. Place the fusible web on top of the fabric, paper side up. Be sure the fabric is larger than the fusible web. To protect your iron, cover the fusible with a nonstick pressing cloth. Follow the manufacturer's instructions to adhere the web to your fabric. Repeat for each piece of the appliqué pattern. Trim on the pattern lines and remove paper backing. Arrange all pieces on an outer shell piece, keeping them at least ¼˝ inside the edge. Iron in place.

Note

All appliqué images have been reversed and are ready for tracing.

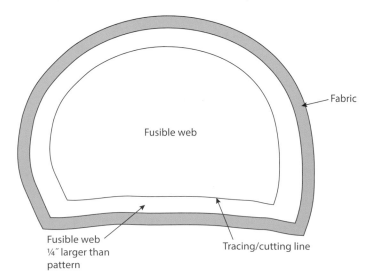

Fabric

Fusible web

Fusible web
¼˝ larger than
pattern

Tracing/cutting line

3. Topstitch around the appliqués approximately ⅛″ from the edges using black thread.

4. If you're making the flower pouch, hand sew the buttons as indicated on the pattern.

5. When the appliqué is finished, it's time to add the zipper. Start with one of the outer shell pieces right side up on your cutting surface. Place the zipper, teeth down, across the top of the fabric with the far edge of the zipper along the edge of the fabric, and so that both ends extend past the edges. Pin in place. (Your zipper might seem too long, but be patient. This technique makes adding a zipper a breeze!) **Fig. A**

6. Place a piece of the lining fabric, right side down, on top of the pinned zipper. Make sure to match the top and side edges of the outer shell and lining. Pin the lining fabric in place. **Fig. B**

7. Sew using the zipper foot on your sewing machine. **Fig. C**

tip

- Dropping the feed dogs on the sewing machine and using a free-motion foot can be helpful but is not necessary.

- If your stitching misses an edge or gets a little wobbly, stitch back over that part. There is nothing wrong with going over the stitches a few times; it adds detail.

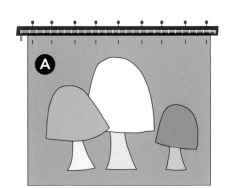

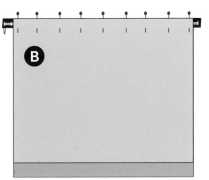

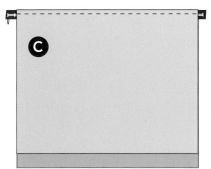

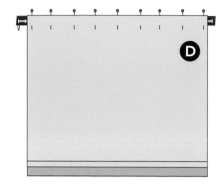

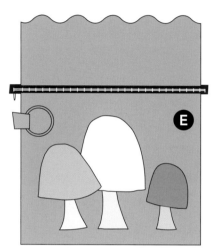

8. Fold the fabric back from the zipper so that the outer shell and lining are wrong sides together. Place the remaining side of the zipper face down onto the right side of the remaining outer shell piece. Align outer shell fabric sides with the fabrics sewn in Step 7. Pin in place. **Fig. D**

9. Place the lining, right side down, on top of the zipper. Make sure to match the top and side edges of the outer shell and lining fabrics. Pin in place and sew.

10. Thread the ribbon through the spilt ring and fold the ribbon in half so that the ends meet and the right side is facing out. Pin together. On the front side of the outer shell, measure approximately 1˝ down from the zipper on the side with the zipper pull. Pin the loop so the ring is toward the center of the bag. **Fig. E**

tip

Make sure the metal ring is in at least ½˝ from the raw edge of the bag, or else it will be in the way when you sew. The ribbon edges are intended to be longer on the inside of the bag; therefore, don't try to align the edges with the raw edges of the bag. The ribbon is longer to ensure that it doesn't come unraveled and come loose from your bag.

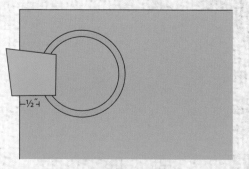

11. If you are using sari ribbon or pom-pom trim, pin it across the bottom of the front of the bag, with the trims facing inward. **Fig. F**

12. Unzip the zipper approximately ⅔ of the way. Place the 2 outer fabrics right sides together and the 2 lining pieces right sides together. When you are ready to pin the zipper sides, fold the zipper in half so that the teeth are on the fold. Make sure the teeth of the zipper are facing the outer bag fabric pieces. **Fig. G**

13. Sew around all of the edges, leaving a 3″ section open at the bottom of the lining for turning. Clip the corners, taking care not to clip the stitching. Cut off all of the excess zipper and trim. **Fig. H**

14. Turn the pouch right side out. Hand stitch the opening closed. Push the lining inside the bag and press.

15. If you're making the camper bag, hand stitch the felt balls onto the bottom.

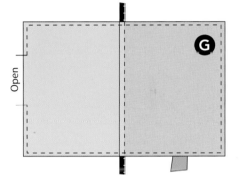

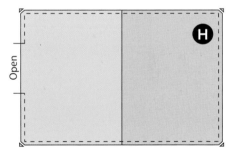

tip

For an extra touch, you can attach ribbons, pom-poms, or beads to the zipper pull.

VARIATION 1

Trimmed and Buttoned Zipper Pouch

Instead of adding an appliqué, sew rows of trims and buttons for one-of-a-kind gifts.

VARIATION 2

Scrappy Flower Zipper Pouch

Substitute Pattern 8 (page 97), Pattern 11 (page 99) and Patterns 35 and 36 (pullout page P1) to make a girly pouch; ruffly tulle and pom-poms across the bottom are a must!

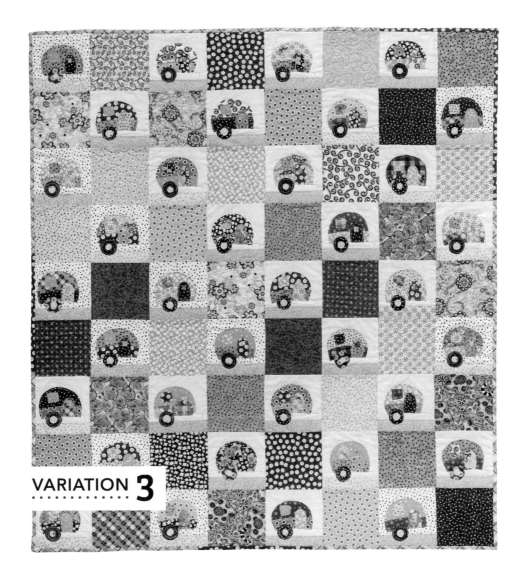

Appliqué Quilt

Follow Steps 1–3 of the Appliqué Zipper Pouches instructions (page 32) and add a 2″ × 6½″ appliqué piece for the ground onto the 6½″ square block and Pattern 1, 2, 3, or 4 (pages 94 and 95) to make as many 6½″ × 6½″ blocks as you need to make the quilt size you want. This quilt is 60″ × 84″; 10 blocks × 14 blocks for 140 blocks total. The camper appliqué is used for 70 blocks, and the other 70 blocks are 6½″ × 6½″ blocks of coordinating fabrics.

Strawberry

PINCUSHION IN A CUP

Sew up a garden-theme pincushion with a fabric strawberry on top. Felt, wool, and floss are all used in this project.

Finished size: approximately 4″ × 7″

MATERIALS

- 1 fat quarter of quilting cotton for pincushion (or 1 square 3 times the diameter of the bowl)

- ¼ yard or fat quarter of red quilting cotton for strawberries

- 6″ × 6″ piece of green felted wool for strawberry caps, flower leaves, and stems

- 4″ × 4″ piece of green felt for bottom layer of strawberry caps

- 2″ × 4″ piece of white felt for flower

- 1cm (approximately ½″) yellow felt ball for flower center

- ⅝ yard ¼″–½″-diameter pom-pom trim

- 2 ounces fiberfill

- Ceramic bowl or cup (A bowl for ice cream or soup measuring 4″–6″ in diameter works best.)

- Hot glue gun and glue sticks

- 5″–6″ doll needle

- All-purpose thread in coordinating colors

- Yellow 6-strand embroidery floss that matches felt ball

For more information about the materials and techniques used in this project, please see Things to Collect (page 12) and Hand Stitching (page 22).

CUTTING

Find strawberry Patterns 15, 16, 17, and 18 and flower Patterns 19 and 20 (pullout page P1).

Red

- 1 small strawberry (#15)

- 1 large strawberry (#16)

Green wool

- 1 small strawberry cap (#17)

- 1 large strawberry cap (#18)

- 2 flower leaves (#19)

- ⅝″ × ⅝″ small strawberry stem

- ¾″ × ¾″ large strawberry stem

Green felt

- 1 small strawberry cap (#17)

- 1 large strawberry cap (#18)

White felt

- 2 flowers (#20)

Fat quarter

- To make the pincushion, measure the diameter of the bowl and multiply by 3 to find the diameter of the circle of fabric you will need to cut. Cut a square to this size and then round the corners to make a circle.

Note

The circle does not have to be perfectly round to work for the pincushion.

Instructions

Seam allowances are ¼˝.

1. Fold the small strawberry piece in half, right sides together, lining up the straight sides of the berry. Using a ¼˝ seam allowance and a straight stitch, sew this side. Turn right side out. Repeat for large strawberry. **Fig. A**

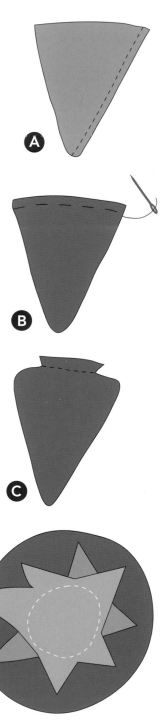

2. Using a needle and thread, run a gathering stitch ¼˝ from the open edge of a berry. Fill with fiberfill and pull the thread snug. Secure with a knot. Repeat for the other berry. **Figs. B & C**

3. Sew a wool and a felt leaf to the top of a berry, covering the gathering stitches, and set aside. Repeat Steps 1–3 for the large strawberry. **Fig. D**

4. Roll the green wool into a stem and hand stitch along the edge to secure. Sew onto the top of the berry leaves. It's okay if the stitches show; it adds detail. Repeat for the other berry. **Fig. E**

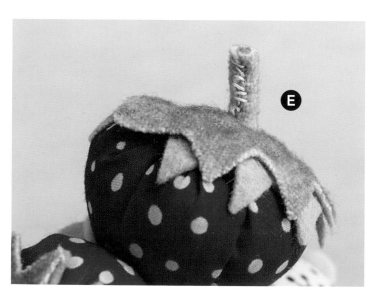

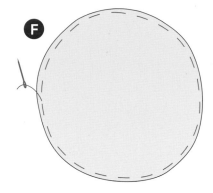

5. For the pincushion, run a gathering stitch ¼″ from the edge. Fill the circle with fiberfill and pull the thread to make a ball shape. Test how it fits into your cup and add or remove fiberfill as needed. **Fig. F**

6. Cut the felt ball in half. Sew 1 half to a felt flower petal. Make 2 of these. **Fig. G**

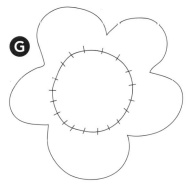

7. Using a doll needle, sew the strawberry to the top of the pincushion. Stitch the second strawberry to the pincushion top as well. Arrange and sew the leaves and 2 flowers onto the top. **Fig. H**

8. Hot glue the pincushion into the cup to secure. **Fig. I**

9. Hot glue the pom-pom trim to the edge of the cup.

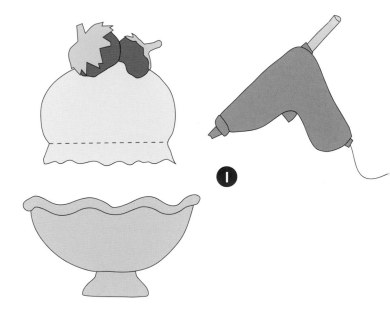

Millinery Pincushion

Make a pincushion in a cup following the Strawberry Pincushion in a Cup instructions (page 40), but then sew on some fun birds, fruit, or other millinery supply for a one-of-a-kind pincushion.

VARIATION **1**

Holiday Pincushion

How about a pincushion for every holiday? Make a pincushion in a cup following the Strawberry Pincushion in a Cup instructions (page 40), but then sew on ornaments, eggs, shamrocks, and so forth.

VARIATION **2**

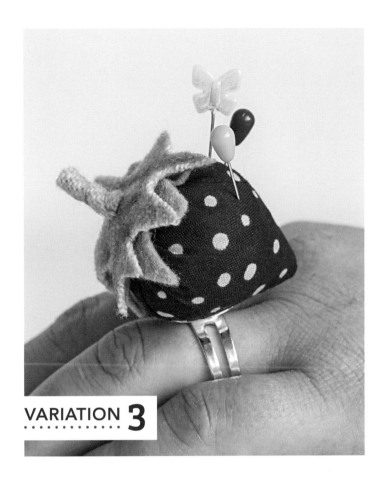

Strawberry Pincushion Ring

Make a small strawberry using Patterns 15 and 17 and following Steps 1–4 of the Strawberry Pincushion in a Cup instructions (page 40). Sew it onto an adjustable ring.

tip

Rings with holes for sewing can be found through jewelry suppliers. They are usually used for seed-bead stitching.

Toadstools on a Log
DRAFT DODGER

A stuffed "log" with toadstools across the top will keep your drafts out in the winter while looking cute.

Finished size: approximately 17″ × 2½″

MATERIALS

- ¼ yard brown quilting cotton for log
- 6″ × 6″ pieces of 5 different quilting cotton prints for the toadstool tops
- 12″ × 12″ piece of cream felt for stems
- 6″ × 6″ piece of green wool for moss
- 6″ × 6″ piece of green felt for grass
- 2″ × 8″ or 4″ × 4″ piece of blue wool for flowers
- Tulle scraps
- 3 yellow felt balls, 1cm (approximately ½″) in diameter
- 4 ounces fiberfill
- *Optional:* ¼ yard or fat quarter of muslin (for weighted bag)
- *Optional:* 1 cup sand or pellets for weight

CUTTING

Find toadstool top Pattern 16, moss Patterns 19 and 21, log end Pattern 22, and flower Pattern 20 (pullout page P1).

Brown

- 1 piece 8½″ × 18″ for log
- 2 log ends (#22)

Print

- 5 toadstool tops (#16)

Cream felt

- 1½″ × 9″ for toadstool stem
- 1½″ × 7″ for toadstool stem
- 1″ × 4″ for toadstool stem
- 1¾″ × 3″ for toadstool stem
- 2¼″ × 3″ for toadstool stem

Green wool

- 2 pieces of moss: 1 (#19) and 1 (#21)

Green felt

- 4 grass pieces cut free-hand: Cut a ½″-wide strip to go around the bottom of the toadstool stem. Cut V-shaped notches in the top long edge to look like grass.

Blue wool

- 3 toadstool flowers (#20)

> For more information about the materials and techniques used in this project, please see Things to Collect (page 12) and Hand Stitching (page 22).

Instructions

Seam allowances are ¼˝.

1. Fold the log fabric lengthwise, right sides together. Sew the long seam, using a straight stitch, leaving a 4˝ opening in the middle of the seam. **Fig. A**

2. Sew the ends onto the log, clip, and turn. **Fig. B**

3. Stuff the log with fiberfill. If you have chosen to place a weighted bag inside, stuff around all of the sides, keeping the bag toward the bottom half of the log. Hand stitch the opening closed and set aside.

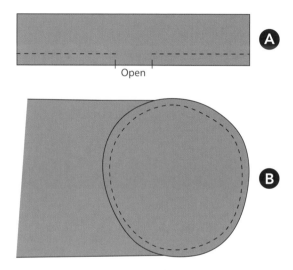

WEIGHTED BAG (*OPTIONAL*)

Cut out 2 rectangles measuring 2˝ × 12˝. Sew together, leaving one end open. Fill this with sand or pellets and sew closed. Don't worry about raw edges or turning; this will be hidden. Tuck this bag into the log.

tip

Keep a bag of play sand around and make little muslin bags for all of your pincushions. This keeps them from moving around when you're using them.

4. Fold a toadstool top in half, right sides together, lining up the straight sides. Using a ¼″ seam allowance and a straight stitch, sew this side, making sure to curve at the top of the cap at the fold line. Turn right side out. Repeat for the other 4 toadstool tops. **Fig. C**

5. To make stems, roll a piece of felt into a stem shape and sew up the side in matching thread to secure. Repeat for all 5 stems. **Figs. D & E**

6. Using a needle and thread, sew a gathering stitch ¼″ from the open edge of the toadstool cap and fill the cap with fiberfill. Start to pull the thread to gather the cap so that the raw edges are turning inward. Place a stem into the opening and then pull the thread to tighten around the felt stem. Stitch around the gather to secure. Make 5 toadstools. **Fig. F**

7. Arrange the toadstools onto the log where you would like them. Stitch down a pieces of moss and then the toadstools. Add grass and tulle.

8. To make flowers, hand sew 1 felt ball to the center of each of the 3 blue wool petals. Hand stitch them to the log where you would like them.

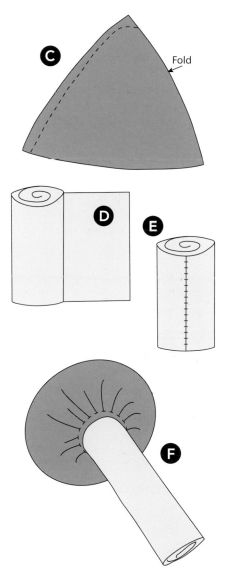

Fold

C

D

E

F

Toadstool Pincushion in a Cup

Make a pincushion in a cup following the Strawberry Pincushion in a Cup instructions (page 40), except add a toadstool instead of a strawberry.

Millinery Draft Dodger

Make a log following the Toadstools on a Log Draft Dodger instructions (page 46), except add a bird or millinery flowers instead.

Scrappy Sewing Machine Pincushion

Make a log following the Toadstools on a Log Draft Dodger instructions (page 46), except make the log shorter and add some fun fabric and trims in rows. Place in front of your sewing machine and you have a nice long pincushion.

tip

Any of these variations could be used as a sewing machine pincushion. Adjust the length of the log's rectangle to the width of the front of your sewing machine for the perfect size.

Little Ones
STUFFED BUNNY

This little bunny will make any little one smile. The cheeks and nose are made from felt balls cut in half.

Finished size: approximately 10˝ × 20˝ (including ears)

MATERIALS

- ¼ yard quilting cotton for body, legs, and outer ears
- ⅛ yard quilting cotton for shorts
- ⅛ yard quilting cotton for hands and shoes
- 8″ × 8″ felt for inner ears
- ¼ yard tulle for skirt
- ⅛ yard quilting cotton for skirt waistband
- 1 yard shoelace ribbon ⅛″–¼″ wide
- ⅓ yard hair ribbon ⅛″–¼″ wide
- 2 black coin beads or buttons (½″) for eyes
- 1″ button for dress flower
- 1″ × 1″ square of green felt for leaf
- 2″ felt ball for cheeks
- 1″ felt ball for nose
- 8 ounces of fiberfill
- White 6-strand floss for whiskers
- All-purpose sewing thread in coordinating colors
- 5″–6″ doll needle

CUTTING

Find Pattern 23 for the bunny body, Pattern 24 for the outer ear, Pattern 25 for shorts, Pattern 26 for the hands and shoes, and Pattern 27 for the inner ear (pullout page P1).

Cutting Note: Be sure to place fabric right sides together when cutting the ears. This will give you 1 piece identical to the pattern piece and 1 piece that is the reverse of the pattern piece. You will need 2 ears that match Pattern 24 and 2 that are reversed.

Body

- 2 body pieces (#23)
- 4 outer ears (#24)
- 2 rectangles 2½″ × 4¾″ for legs

Shorts

- 2 shorts pieces (#25)

Hand and shoes

- 4 hands and 4 shoes (#26)

Inner ears

- 2 inner ears (#27)

Skirt

- 5″ × 40″ from tulle
- 3″ × 24″ from cotton

Flower leaf

- 1 leaf for the button flower cut freehand

For more information about the materials and techniques used in this project, please see Things to Collect (page 12) and Attaching Embellishments (page 20).

Instructions

Seam allowances are ¼″.

1. Separate 4 ear pieces into 2 pairs, right sides together, matching the bottom curve. Position so that the sides marked *inside* are next to each other. Take the top piece from each stack and place it faceup. Place a felt inner ear piece on top of each ear, matching the bottom curve. Topstitch each inner ear piece to an ear using coordinating thread. **Fig. A**

2. With right sides together sew both sets of ears together. Leave the bottom open. Clip the curves. Turn and press from the back (the side without the felt inner ear). **Fig. B**

3. Sew the hands to the arms as indicated on the pattern piece. Sew the shoes to the legs. Press the seams. **Fig. C**

4. Place the leg sets right sides together, matching the shoe seams. Sew around the outside, leaving the end opposite the feet open for turning. Clip the curves, turn, press, and lightly fill with fiberfill. **Fig. D**

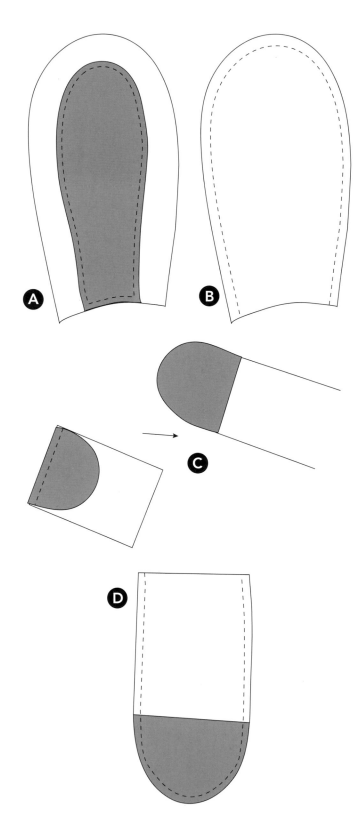

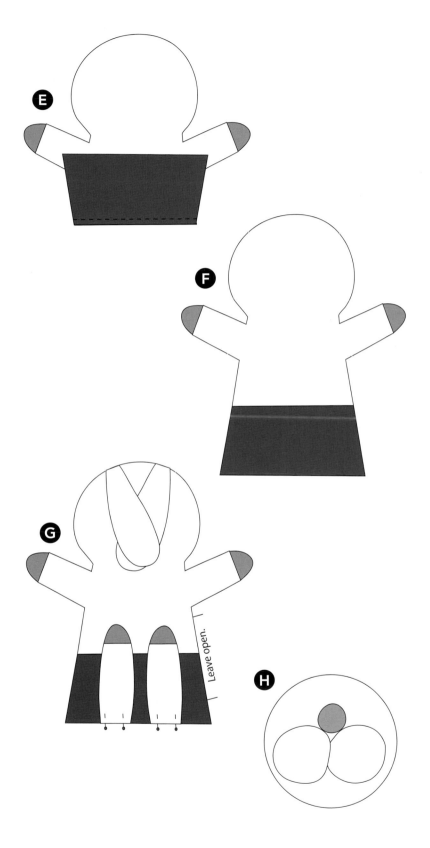

5. Sew a shorts piece to each of the bunny body pieces and press the seam. **Figs. E & F**

6. Following the diagram, pin the legs and ears onto the body so that they are facing inward. Place the remaining body piece on top. Sew, starting just under one arm, then around the body and across the bottom, leaving an opening on the side for turning. **Fig. G**

7. Clip, turn, and fill with fiberfill. Hand stitch the opening closed.

8. Topstitch the arms where they meet the bunny body to allow them to move.

9. The side of the bunny with the felt on the ears is the front of your bunny. Cut the large felt ball in half with scissors. These are the cheeks; arrange onto the face and hand stitch in place. Stitch the felt ball on for the nose. **Fig. H**

10. Sew on the eyes using black thread. Refer to the diagram for placement.

11. To make whiskers, use floss doubled up and a long doll needle. Go in one side of the cheeks and out the other. Tie a knot with the 2 strands on either side of the cheeks to secure. Trim the excess thread and repeat 2 more times. **Fig. I**

12. Use hair ribbon to tie a bow with 1 or 2 ribbons and tack in place above an ear. **Fig. J**

13. Cut shoe ribbon in half. Wrap one piece of the shoe ribbon around one foot and tie a bow. Trim the excess ribbon and repeat on the second shoe. Tack in place at the back of the shoe. **Fig. K**

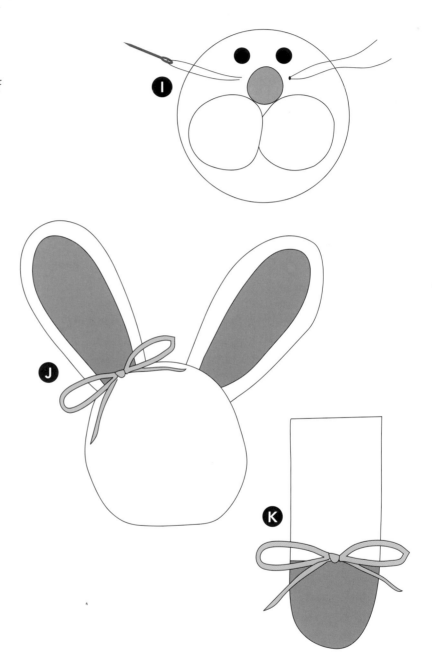

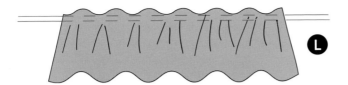

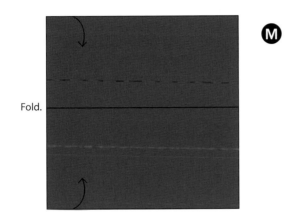

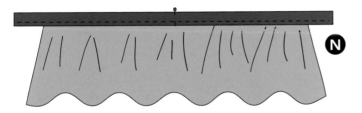

14. Hand sew a gathering stitch along the long side of the tulle. Gently pull the tulle so that it measures approximately 12˝. **Fig. L**

15. Fold the waistband fabric in half lengthwise, wrong sides together, and press. Open up and fold raw edges in to the center line and press. Refold the first fold. **Fig. M**

16. Find the center and mark with a pin. Find the center of the tulle and align with the marked pin. Slide the tulle into the fold and pin the tulle in place. Topstitch the open edge from one end of the waist-band to the other, catching the tulle in the fold. Wrap the skirt around the bunny and tie a bow in the back. **Fig. N**

17. Layer the felt leaf and the button and sew together. Stitch this to the bunny's skirt. **Fig. O**

tip
Doll-making needles are extra long and they are very useful when making stuffies.

Boy Bunny

Make the bunny following the Little Ones Stuffed Bunny instructions (page 52), except leave off the tulle skirt and flower hair bow and add 2 buttons to the pants.

Tooth Fairy Pillow

Make the bunny following the Little Ones Stuffed Bunny instructions (page 52) and hand stitch a felt pocket to the bunny's tummy using Pattern 26 on the pattern pullout page.

Cat Stuffie

Swap out the bunny ears for the cat ears and you have
a whole new animal. Make the bunny following the Little
Ones Stuffed Bunny instructions (page 52), except replace
the bunny ears with Patterns 28 and 29 for the inner and
outer cat ears on the pattern pullout page.

Flower
WALLHANGING

This cute wallhanging features a large, bright flower appliqué surrounded with buttons and includes felt balls across the bottom. It is a cheery addition to any decor.

Finished size: approximately 12″ × 16″ without felt ball bottom trim

MATERIALS

- ⅜ yard quilting cotton for background

- ⅛ yard or fat quarter quilting cotton for grass and leaf

- ¼ yard, fat quarter, or 9″ × 9″ square quilting cotton for outer flower circle

- ¼ yard, fat quarter, or 8″ × 8″ square quilting cotton for large middle circle

- ¼ yard, fat eighth, or 6½″ × 6½″ square quilting cotton for small middle circle

- ⅛ yard, fat eighth, or a 4½″ × 4½″ square quilting cotton for small center circle

- ⅛ yard, fat eighth, or 3½″ × 6½″ quilting cotton for stem

- ½ yard quilting cotton for backing and binding

- 7 felt balls, 2cm (approximately 1″) in diameter in coordinating colors

- Approximately 26 buttons, ½″–¾″

- ⅜ yard batting

- ⅔ yard paper-backed fusible web (17″ wide)

- Coordinating thread

- 3-strand floss, green and 2 coordinating colors

- All-purpose sewing thread in coordinating colors

- Nonstick pressing cloth

> For more information about the materials and techniques used in this project, please see Things to Collect (page 12) and Attaching Embellishments (page 20).

CUTTING

Find and trace Patterns 5, 6, 7, and 8 for flower circles; Pattern 9 for stem; and Pattern 10 for leaf (pages 96–98).

Note

All appliqué images have been reversed and are ready for tracing.

Background
- 12″ × 13½″

Grass
- 3″ × 12″

Backing
- 14″ × 18″

Binding
- 4 strips 2½″ × 18″

Batting
- 14″ × 18″

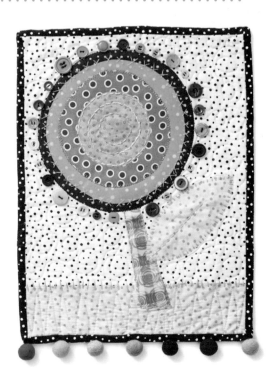

Instructions

Seam allowances are ¼″.

1. Sew the long edge of the grass to a short edge of the background. Press the seam. **Fig. A**

2. Trace the flower circles, leaf, and stem appliqués onto the paper side of the fusible web.

3. Cut out the fusible web approximately ¼″ outside the drawn line. Place the appliqué fabric right side down on the ironing board. Place the fusible web on top of the fabric, paper side up. Be sure the fabric is larger than the fusible web. To protect your iron, cover the fusible web with a non-stick pressing cloth. Follow the manufacturer's instructions to adhere the web to your fabric. Repeat for each piece. Trim on the pattern lines and remove the paper backing.

4. Arrange all pieces following the diagram, beginning with the stem. Next, layer on the leaf and large outer flower circle. Iron in place. Add the smaller circles one at a time. **Fig. B**

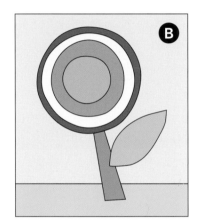

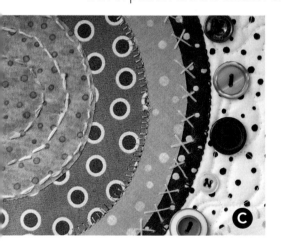

5. Using the buttonhole stitch, sew around the edges of the large outer circle and the small middle circle appliqués using coordinating thread. **Fig. C**

6. Using floss, hand stitch around the edge of the large middle circle making fun X's. **Fig. D**

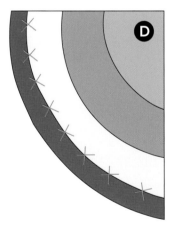

tip

Cross-stitch and running stitch instructions are in Embroidery (page 23).

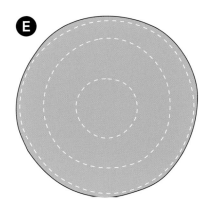

7. Stitch 3 circles using the running stitch and floss in the small circle. **Fig. E**

8. With the green floss, use a running stitch to sew around the stem, to make grass, and to sew around the leaf. **Fig. F**

9. Stack the backing, batting, and top together and quilt the background of this quilt.

10. Trim the batting and background to match. Sew binding strips together to make a long strip 2½″ wide. Use your favorite technique to bind the quilt.

11. Hand stitch felt balls across the bottom. **Fig. G**

12. Using the black floss, attach buttons around the outer edge of the flower. **Fig. H**

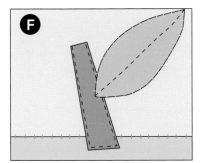

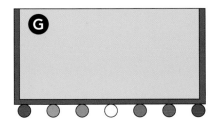

tip

If the hand stitching scares you away from this project, use your machine and a buttonhole stitch for all of the stitching.

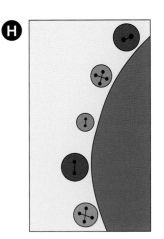

Bull's-Eye Pillows

Make the pillow using Patterns 5, 6, 7, and 8 (pages 96 and 97) and paper-backed fusible web to add the appliqués for the bull's-eyes to the front, following the manufacturer's instructions. Cut the pillow front square at least 6″ larger than the largest circle appliqué. Follow Steps 1–4 of the Pom-Pom Pillow instructions (page 90), cutting 2 pieces for the back to be 3 1/2″ wider than the front to allow for the button and buttonhole bands. Hand stitch felt balls around the edges for fun.

VARIATION 1

> ### tip
>
> If you want to make more rings on your pillows, look around the house for bowls and plates to trace for larger circles.

Trivet

Use Patterns 5, 6, 7, and 8 (pages 96 and 97) to make and stitch the appliqué circles to a larger circle. Cut a circle of batting and backing. Layer the top and backing, rights sides together, and add the batting to the top of the stack. Sew around the outside edge, leaving an opening for turning. Trim, clip curves, and turn right side out, making sure the batting is between the fabric layers. Hand stitch the opening closed. Stitch felt balls around the outer edge.

VARIATION 2

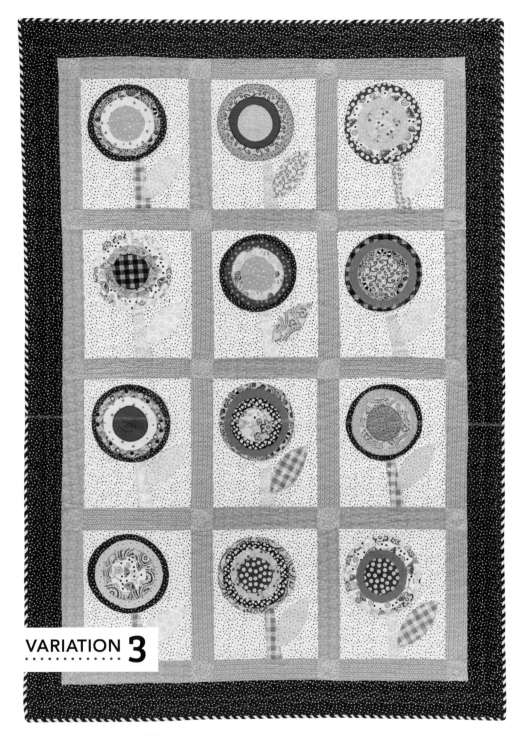

VARIATION 3

Flower Quilt

Make 12 quilt blocks following Steps 1–6 of the Flower Wallhanging instructions (page 60). Sew 12 blocks together with 3″ sashing and cornerstones between the vertical rows. Add borders, and then follow Steps 7 and 8 to finish.

Mocha
MUG RUG

Add an embroidered and embellished mocha cup, stitching, yo-yos, buttons, and trims to these cute mug rugs. This is a great project for using up that pile of fabric scraps. Perfect for the office. Make lots for gifts!

Finished size:
6¼″ × 9½″

MATERIALS

- ¼ yard, fat eighth, or 6″ × 8″ scrap of quilting cotton for background
- ¼ yard, fat quarter, or 12″ × 12″ scrap of quilting cotton for table and backing
- Fabric scraps for appliqués and yo-yos
- 6 pieces 2½″ × 4″ for side border
- 2 pieces of trim 8″ long
- 8″ × 12″ piece of batting
- 10″ × 10″ piece of fusible web
- 2 buttons ranging from ¼″ to 1″
- 6-strand black or brown floss
- Nonstick pressing cloth

For more information about the materials and techniques used in this project, please see Things to Collect (page 12) and Attaching Embellishments (page 20).

CUTTING

Find the small and large yo-yos, Patterns 30 and 31 (pullout page P1). Use Pattern 12 (page 99) for the cup.

Background

- 5¼″ × 7″

Table and backing

- 2″ × 7″
- 6¾″ × 10″

Batting

- 6¾″ × 10″

Yo-yos

- 1 (#30)
- 1 (#31)

Instructions

Seam allowances are ¼˝.

1. With right sides together, sew background to table along a 7˝ side. Press seam.

2. Trace the cup appliqués onto the paper side of the fusible web.

3. Cut out the fusible web approximately ¼˝ outside the drawn line. Place the appliqué fabric right side down on the ironing board. Place the fusible web on top of the fabric, paper side up. Be sure the fabric is larger than the fusible web. To protect your iron, cover the fusible web with a non-stick pressing cloth. Follow the manufacturer's instructions to adhere the web to your fabric. Repeat for each piece of the appliqué pattern. Trim on the pattern lines and remove paper backing. Arrange all the background and tabletop pieces. Iron in place.

4. Sew around the outside appliqué edges and table top with black thread. Stitch steam above the cup. **Fig. A**

5. Hand stitch the word *Mocha* onto the cup. **Fig. B**

6. Sew the 2½˝ × 4˝ strips together at different angles. Press each seam as you go, taking care to ensure that the strip doesn't curve to one side. **Fig. C**

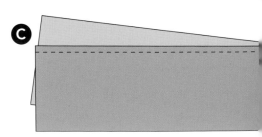

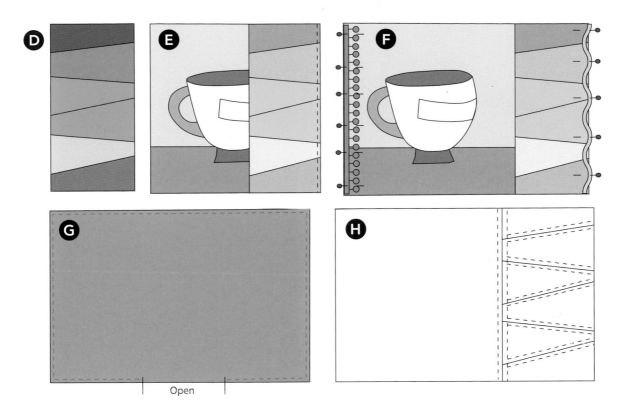

tip

Clover has a yo-yo tool that makes them easy to create.

7. Press the seams flat and trim to 3½″ × 6¾″. **Fig. D**

8. Sew the scrappy strip to the appliqué block and press. **Fig. E**

9. Pin a trim to each of the shorter sides of the mug rug, making sure the trim edges are pointing inward. **Fig. F**

10. Place the backing and appliqué right sides together. Place batting on top and stitch around the outer edge, leaving a 3″ gap along the bottom for turning. **Fig. G**

11. Clip the corners, turn, and press. Quilt each side of the seam where the block meets the scrappy strip and within the strips. Hand stitch the opening closed. **Fig. H**

12. To make yo-yos, fold ¼″ of fabric to the wrong side and finger-press. Sew a gathering stitch around the top, going through both layers of fabric. Pull to gather. Tie a knot in the thread to secure. Sew the yo-yos, along with 2 buttons, to the top of the mug rug.

VARIATION **1**

Happy Camper Mug Rug

Follow the Mocha Mug Rug instructions (page 66), substituting Pattern 2 (page 94) camper appliqué for the coffee cup.

VARIATION **2**

Mocha Coasters

Follow the Mocha Mug Rug instructions (page 66), leaving off the scrappy side border, and make coasters. Add trim to all 4 sides.

VARIATION **3**

Mocha Zipper Pouch

Make a pouch following the Appliqué Zipper Pouches instructions (page 32), using Pattern 12 (page 99) for the coffee cup appliqué to hold your coffee change.

Happy Scrappy
PLACE MATS

Add loads of trims, fabric flaps, and a flower to embellish these bright, quilted place mats. Make some for every holiday and season.

Finished size: approximately 13″ × 17″ (without flaps)

MATERIALS

Makes 4 place mats.

- 2⅝ yards quilting cotton for front, back, and binding
- 36″ × 42″ piece of batting
- Fabric scraps for flaps measuring 6″ × 8″ or larger (total of 1¼ yards of scraps)
- 2 yards each of 4 trims
- 12 felt, fabric, and velvet scraps each measuring 4″ × 4″ (for 4 flowers)
- 12″ × 12″ piece of green felt for leaves
- 4 buttons, 1″ diameter
- All-purpose thread in coordinating colors

> For more information about the materials and techniques used in this project, please see Things to Collect (page 12) and Attaching Embellishments (page 20).

CUTTING

Find small flap Pattern 33, large flap Pattern 32, flower Pattern 34, and flower circle Patterns 31 and 35 (pullout page P1).

Front and back
- 2 pieces 36″ × width of fabric (selvages removed)

Flaps
- 44 small flaps (#33)
- 44 large flaps (#32)

Flowers
- 4 small circles (#35)
- 4 flowers (#34)
- 4 large circles (#31)

Green felt
- 4 leaves cut freehand

Binding
- 7 strips 2½″ × width of fabric (selvages removed)

Instructions

Seam allowances are ¼˝.

1. With right sides together, sew 22 sets of large flaps and 22 sets of small flaps, leaving the straight edges open. Clip the curves, turn right side out, and press. **Fig. A**

2. Trim batting even with top and backing fabric pieces. Make a quilt sandwich by placing the backing fabric right side down, cover with batting, and place top fabric right side up on the top. Smooth sandwich and pin every 3˝ or 4˝. Quilt the entire quilt sandwich. Use a walking foot, if you have one, to prevent the layers from shifting. I chose to quilt wavy lines horizontally.

3. Cut the quilt into 4 place mats measuring 13˝ × 17˝. Sew the desired trims down each side of the mats, starting 1˝ in from the side edge, to allow room for binding later. **Fig. B**

4. Measure ½˝ down from the top and ½˝ up from the bottom of the short sides of each place mat. Mark with pins. **Fig. C**

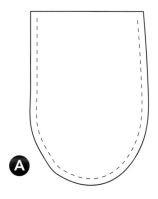

A

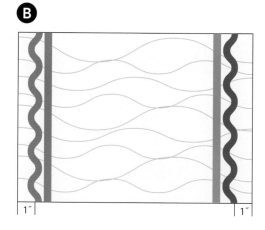

B

1˝ 1˝

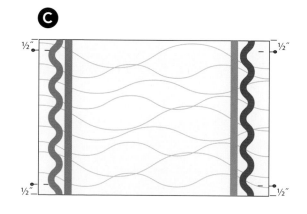

C

½˝ ½˝

½˝ ½˝

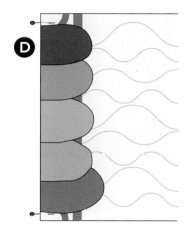

5. Arrange and pin the sewn flaps to each side of the place mat within the pin-marked area matching the raw edges. These flaps will overlap in places. Use 5 flaps on one side of each mat and 6 on the other. **Fig. D**

6. Sew binding strips together to make a long 2½˝-wide strip. Fold in half lengthwise, wrong sides together. Press. Open and fold raw edges in to meet in the center of the strip. Press. Refold original fold.

7. Pin and sew the binding around the entire outside of the place mat. Press and fold the free binding edge to the back of the place mat and hand sew in place. Repeat for the other 3. **Fig. E**

8. Layer the flower pieces. Add a button on top and sew through all of the layers. Add a felt leaf and then sew it to the place mat. **Fig. F**

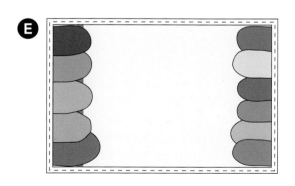

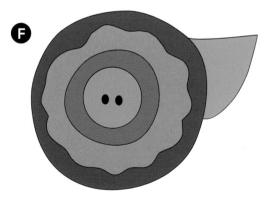

VARIATION **1**

Happy Scrappy Pillow

Make 2 quilted place mats following Steps 1–5 and 8 of the Happy Scrappy Place Mats instructions (page 72). Place the right sides together; sew around the edge, leaving an opening for turning. Turn right side out, stuff, and hand stitch the opening closed.

VARIATION **2**

Happy Scrappy Table Runner

Measure your table and sew pieces of fabric together to make 2 pieces the width and length you want. Follow Steps 1, 2, and 4–7 of the Happy Scrappy Place Mats instructions (page 72). Add trims along the ends.

VARIATION **3**

Happy Scrappy Tote Bag

Make a tote bag following the Embellished Tote Bag instructions (page 78). Add flaps and a flower using Patterns 31, 32, 33, 34, and 35 (pullout page P1). Follow Step 1 of the Happy Scrappy Place Mats instructions (page 72) to make flaps, and then add trims to the bag body. Complete the bag according to the Embellished Tote Bag instructions (page 78), include the flaps across the bottom seam in Step 7. Follow Step 8 of the Happy Scrappy Place Mats instructions (page 78) to make the flower embellishment and sew onto the bag.

Embellished
TOTE BAG

Make this wonderful tote with yo-yos, buttons, and pom-pom flowers in your favorite colors.

Finished size:
14″ × 16″
without handles

MATERIALS

- ½ yard quilting cotton for bag body
- ½ yard quilting cotton for lining
- Pink scraps for 11 yo-yos (about 4″ × 4″ each)
- 2″ × 6″ piece of pink felt for flower petals
- 2″ × 6″ piece of white felt for flower petals
- 3 felt balls, 2cm in diameter
- 25–35 buttons assorted sizes and colors
- Pink 6-strand embroidery floss
- 2 sew-on bag handles
- All-purpose sewing thread in coordinating colors

For more information about the materials and techniques used in this project, please see Things to Collect (page 12) and Attaching Embellishments (page 20).

CUTTING

Find flower Pattern 20 and yo-yo Patterns 30 and 31 (pullout sheet P1). Find and trace heart Pattern 14 (page 101).

Body

- 1 piece 18″ × 20″ (Trim to size after the embroidery is finished on the front piece.)
- 1 piece 14½″ × 16½″

Lining

- 2 pieces 14½″ × 16½″

Yo-yos

- 6 small yo-yos (#30)
- 5 large yo-yos (#31)

Flower petals

- 3 flowers (#20) from white felt
- 2 flowers (#20) from pink felt

Instructions

Seam allowances are ¼˝.

1. Trace the heart onto the center of the 18˝ × 20˝ piece of body fabric.

2. Using 6-strand embroidery floss and a running stitch, sew on the traced line, outlining the heart. Sew a second outline about ¼˝ outside the first line. **Fig. A**

3. To make a flower, cut a felt ball in half. Stitch half of a felt ball to a flower petal piece. Make 5. **Fig. B**

4. To make yo-yos, fold ¼˝ of fabric to the wrong side and finger-press. Sew a gathering stitch around the top, going through both layers of fabric. Pull to gather. Tie a knot in the thread to secure. **Fig. C**

5. Arrange and sew a few yo-yos and felt flowers on the heart. Fill in areas with buttons, remaining yo-yos, and flowers. **Fig. D**

6. Center the heart and trim the body piece to 14½˝ × 16½˝. **Fig. E**

7. Cut a 1¾˝ × 1¾˝ square from each of the bottom corners. **Fig. F**

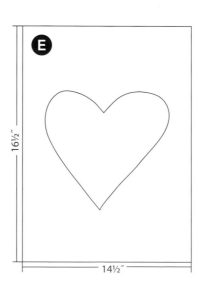

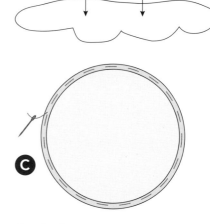

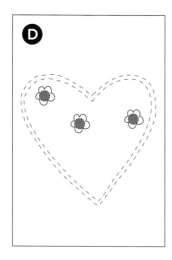

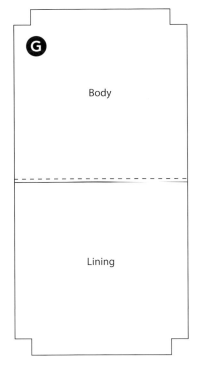

G

Body

Lining

8. Place 1 body and 1 lining piece right sides together. Sew along the top edge, joining the lining and the body. Repeat for the remaining body and lining pieces. Open the pieces and press the seams. **Fig. G**

9. Align the pieces with right sides facing, matching body and lining pieces. Pin and sew, leaving the notched corners open. Leave a 4″ gap at the bottom of the lining for turning. **Fig. H**

10. Open the notched corners. Match lining side and bottom seams at one corner. Pin. Sew to create a box bottom. Repeat for the other lining corner and for both outer fabric corners. **Fig. I**

11. Turn right side out. Hand stitch the opening in the lining closed. Push the lining down into the bag and press. Topstitch ¼″ from the edge.

12. Arrange the bag handles onto the outside of the bag and stitch into place. **Fig. J**

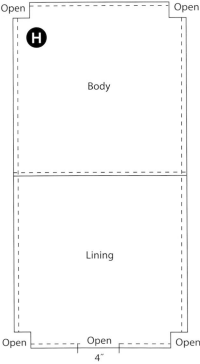

Open   Open

H

Body

Lining

Open   Open   Open
           4″

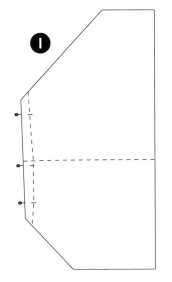

I

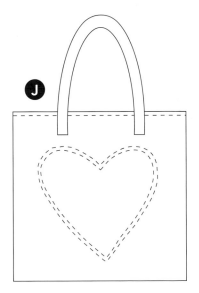

J

tip

Be sure to press the top edge really well to make a nice crease.

Appliqué Bag

Make a tote bag following the Embellished Tote Bag instructions (page 78), except add Pattern 1, 2, 3, or 4 (pages 94 and 95) instead of the heart.

Scrappy Circles Bag

Make a tote bag following the Embellished Tote Bag instructions (page 78), except add a variety of layered circles using Patterns 31, 35, or 36 on the pattern pullout page, and then add button centers.

VARIATION 3

Embellished Pillow

Follow Steps 1–5 of the Embellished Tote Bag instructions (page 78) to make the pillow front. Finish the pillow following Steps 1–9 of the Pom-Pom Pillow instructions (page 90).

Scrappy Stars
WALL QUILT

Brightly colored stars are appliquéd and layered with scrappy fabric circles. The stacks are topped off with a button.

Finished size: approximately 30″ × 36″

MATERIALS

- 1 yard quilting cotton for block background
- 1½ yards total of quilting cotton in red, white, blue, and gold scraps for circles and stars
- 1¼ yards quilting cotton for backing
- ⅜ yard quilting cotton for binding
- 1⅛ yards of batting or a crib-size batting
- 1¾ yards of paper-backed fusible web 17″ wide
- 30 buttons approximately ¾″–1″
- All-purpose sewing thread in coordinating colors
- Nonstick pressing cloth

> For more information about the materials and techniques used in this project, please see Things to Collect (page 12) and Attaching Embellishments (page 20).

CUTTING

Find circle Patterns 31, 35, and 36 (pullout sheet P1) and star Pattern 13 (page 100).

Block background

- 30 squares 6½″ × 6½″

Backing

- 36″ × 42″

Binding

- 4 strips 2½″ × width of fabric (selvages removed)

Circles

- 30 sets of circles

Batting

- 36″ × 42″

Instructions

Seam allowances are ¼˝.

1. Trace 30 star appliqués onto the paper side of the fusible web.

2. Cut out the fusible web approximately ¼˝ outside the drawn line. Place the appliqué fabric right side down on the ironing board. Place the fusible web on top of the fabric, paper side up. Be sure the fabric is larger than the fusible web. To protect your iron, cover the fusible web with a nonstick pressing cloth. Follow the manufacturer's instructions to adhere the web to your fabric. Trim on the pattern lines and remove paper backing.

3. Fuse a star to each of the quilt blocks, making sure each star is at least ¼˝ from the edge of the block background fabric. **Fig. A**

4. Sew 5 blocks together to make a row. Make 6 rows.

5. Sew the 6 rows together to complete the quilt top.

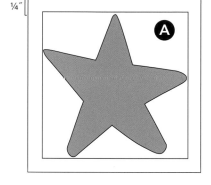

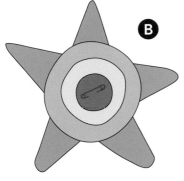

6. Arrange a large circle on top of each star. Safety pin in place. **Fig. B**

7. Sandwich the top, batting, and backing together for your quilt. Safety pin every 3″–4″. Sew around each star. Sew a spiral or a circle through the middle of the circle to secure. Quilt the background as desired.

8. Sew binding strips together to make a long 2½″-wide strip. Fold in half, wrong sides together. Press. Open and fold raw edges in to meet in the center of the strip. Press. Refold original fold.

9. Trim the batting and backing to size and bind the quilt.

10. Hand stitch a button and the two remaining circles to the center of each star. **Fig. C**

tip

Washing the quilt will give the circles a nice scrappy look and frayed edges. After the quilt is washed and dried, trim loose threads.

Scrappy Star Table Runner

Measure your table and cut 2 pieces of fabric the width and length desired. Add the stars and circles from the Scrappy Stars Wall Quilt (page 82) to each end. Follow Steps 2, 6, and 7 of the Happy Scrappy Place Mats instructions (page 72) .

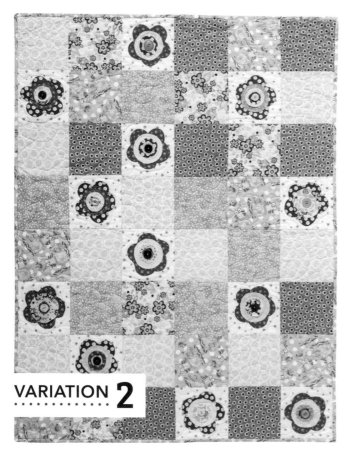

VARIATION **2**

Flower Appliqué Quilt

Make a quilt following the Scrappy Stars Wall Quilt instructions (page 84), except add the appliqués to only some of the blocks, replacing the stars with flowers using Pattern 11 (page 99) and circle Patterns 31, 35, and 36 (pullout page P1).

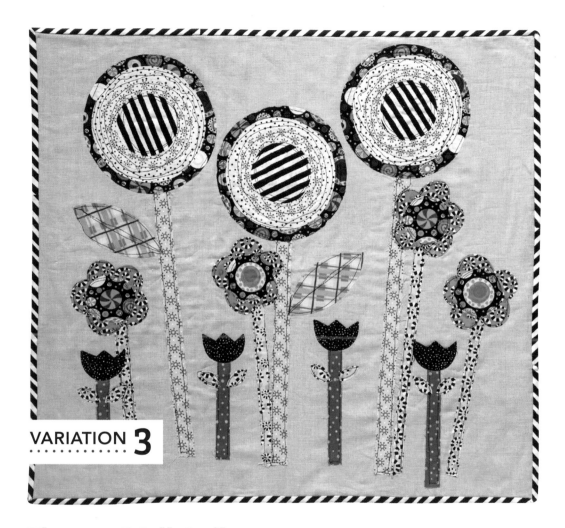

VARIATION 3

Flowers Wall Quilt

Cut the top, backing, and batting pieces 40″ × 50″. Use Patterns 5, 6, 7, 8, and 10 (pages 96–98) for the circle flower and large leaves, Pattern 4 (page 95) for the tulips and small leaves, and Patterns 8 (page 97) and 11 (page 99) for the medium-size flowers. Freehand cut the stems. Create a wallhanging by arranging and appliquéing the flowers onto the quilt top, using the photo for reference. Quilt and bind following Steps 7–9 of the Scrappy Stars Wall Quilt (page 84). This wallhanging measures 36″ × 46″.

Pom-Pom
PILLOW

This fun, whimsical pillow has pom-poms galore!

Finished size:
12″ × 18″

MATERIALS

- ¾ yard quilting cotton for pillow front and back
- 20 pom-poms or 3–5 colors of yarn to make them yourself (see Step 5, page 90)
- 3 buttons 1˝ in diameter
- 12˝ × 18˝ pillow form
- All-purpose sewing thread in coordinating colors

For more information about the materials and techniques used in this project, please see Things to Collect (page 12) and Hand Stitching (page 22).

CUTTING

Pillow front

- 1 rectangle 12½˝ × 18½˝

Pillow back

- 1 rectangle 12½˝ × 17˝
- 1 rectangle 12½˝ × 5˝

Instructions

Seam allowances are ¼˝.

1. Press under ½˝ along the 12½˝ edge of a backing piece. Press under another 1˝ and topstitch this edge. Repeat for the other backing piece. **Fig. A**

2. Make 3 buttonholes on the folded edge of one of the backing pieces, placing the outer buttonholes about 1˝ away from the raw edge. Stitch buttons on the folded edge of the remaining backing piece to align with the buttonholes. **Figs. B & C**

3. Overlap and button the 2 backing pieces to create a 12½˝ × 18½˝ rectangle. Trim if necessary.

4. With right sides together, pin the pillow top and back together. Sew using a ¼˝ seam allowance around all 4 edges. Trim corners. Turn right side out and press. **Fig. D**

5. To make pom-poms, cut a length of corrugated cardboard the width of the pom-poms. For this project, a 1½˝ × 6˝ piece of cardboard was used.

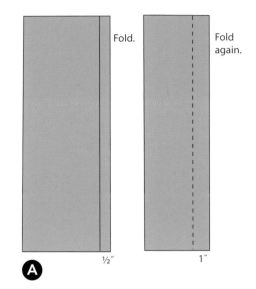

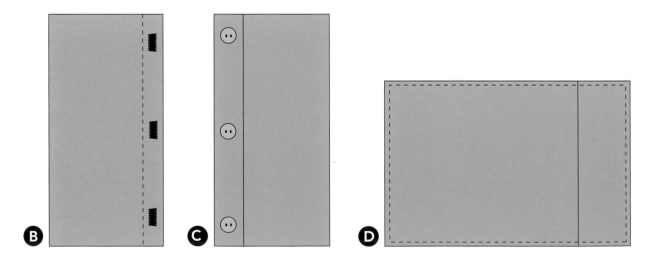

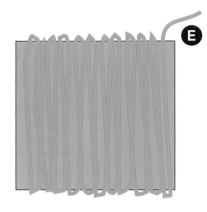

6. Wrap the yarn around the cardboard approximately 40–50 times, depending on the thickness of your yarn. **Fig. E**

7. Carefully slide the yarn off the cardboard and tie a piece of yarn around the center. Make sure to pull it tight. **Fig. F**

8. Cut the yarn loops. Trim to make the pom-pom round.

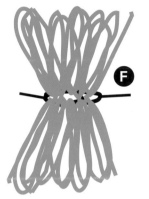

> ## tip
>
> Clover makes a great set of pom-pom makers that creates really even and nice pom-poms, and they don't wear out like the cardboard will.

9. Sew a pom-pom onto each corner of the pillow.

10. Sew on the remaining pom-poms, spacing those on the short sides 4˝ apart and those on the long sides 4½˝ apart.

11. Insert the pillow form.

Pom-Pom Pincushion

Make a 6˝ × 6˝ pillow following Step 4 in Pom-Pom Pillow (page 90), except cut the pillow front and back pieces 6½˝ × 6½˝, leave an opening for turning, stuff with fiberfill, and hand stitch the opening closed. Then follow Steps 5–9 to make and add small pom-poms to the corners and sew a button in the middle.

VARIATION 1

Pom-Pom Garland

Using 6˝ × 6˝ squares of fabric as flags, use Pattern 2 (page 94) to appliqué campers to the right side of the squares. Fold the top of the flag over ½˝ and sew along the long edge to create a channel for cording. Follow Steps 5–9 in Pom-Pom Pillow (page 90) to make pom-poms. String onto cording, alternating with the flags.

VARIATION 2

Pom-Pom Hair Flowers

Use Patterns 31, 34, and 35 (pullout page P1) to make these hair clips.
Add ribbon, tulle, and a pom-pom on top for added fun.

Appliqué Patterns

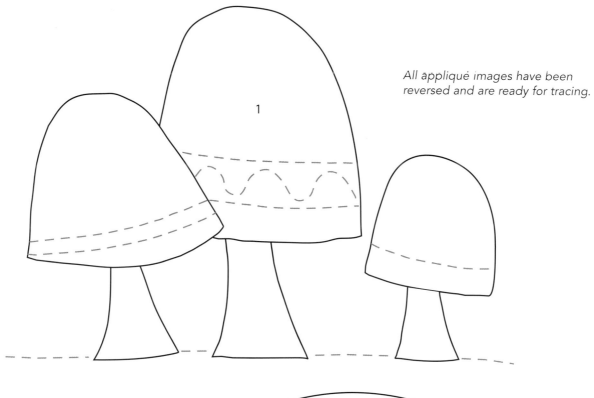

All appliqué images have been reversed and are ready for tracing.

1

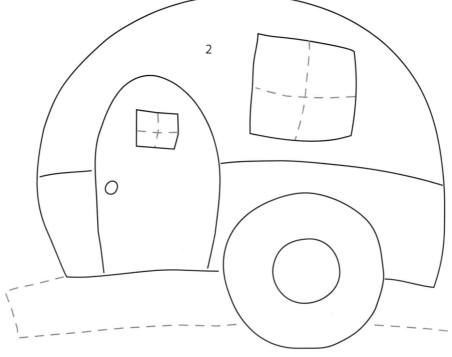

2

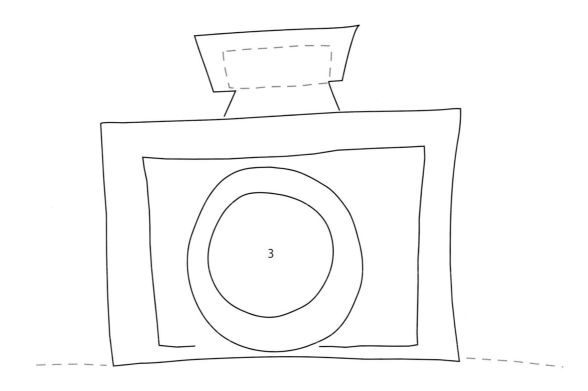

3

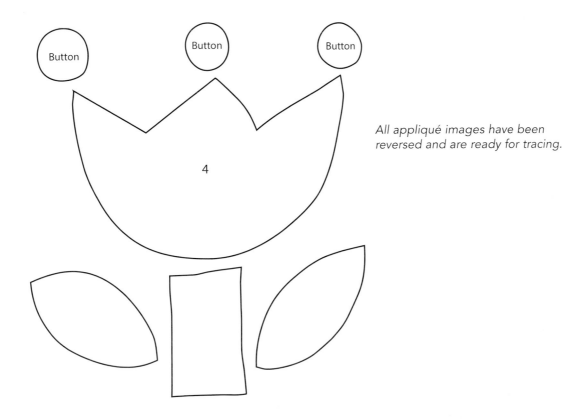

Button

Button

Button

4

All appliqué images have been reversed and are ready for tracing.

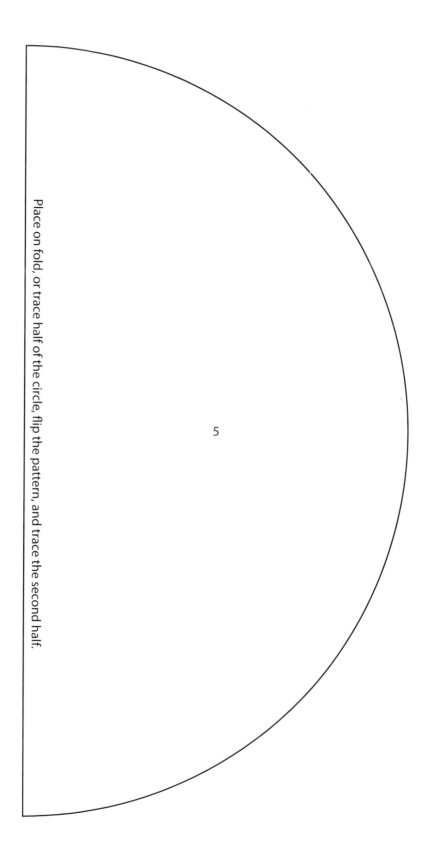

Place on fold, or trace half of the circle, flip the pattern, and trace the second half.

5

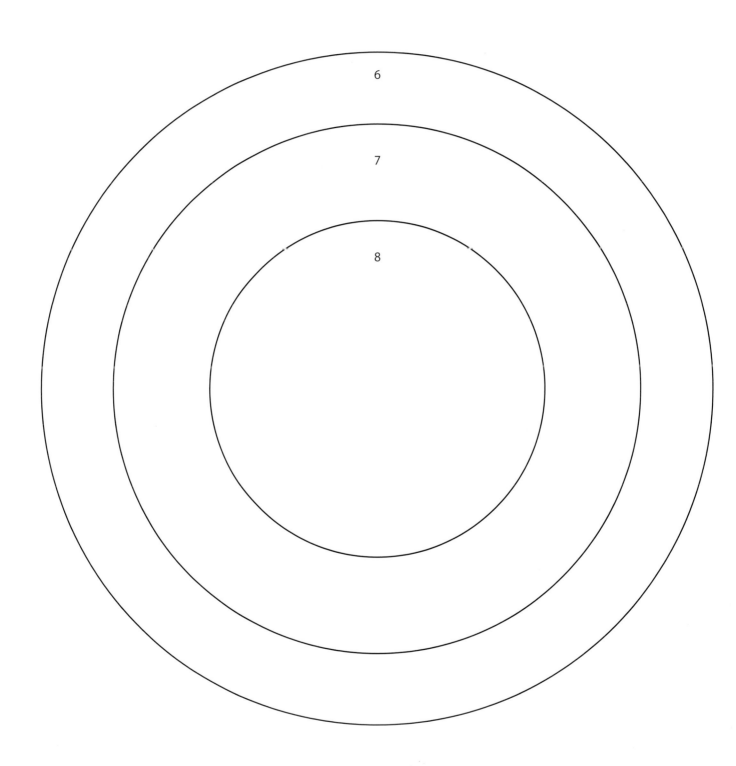

6

7

8

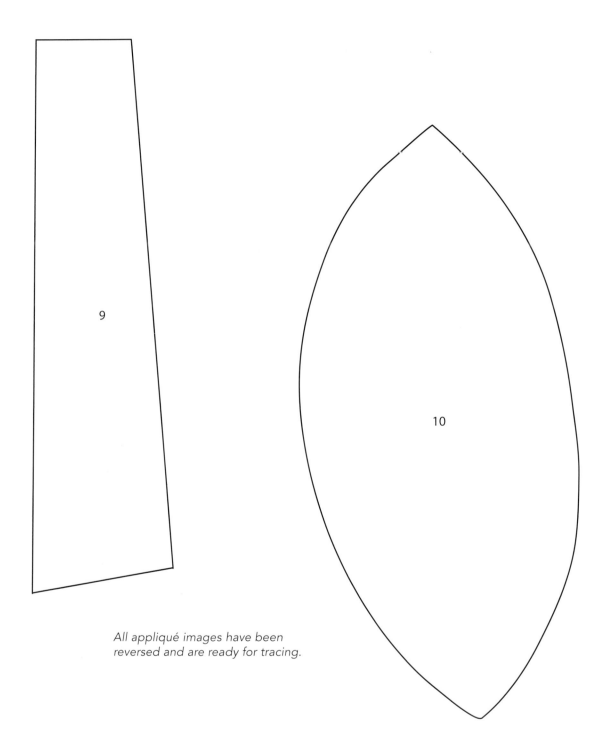

9

10

*All appliqué images have been
reversed and are ready for tracing.*

11

All appliqué images have been reversed and are ready for tracing.

12

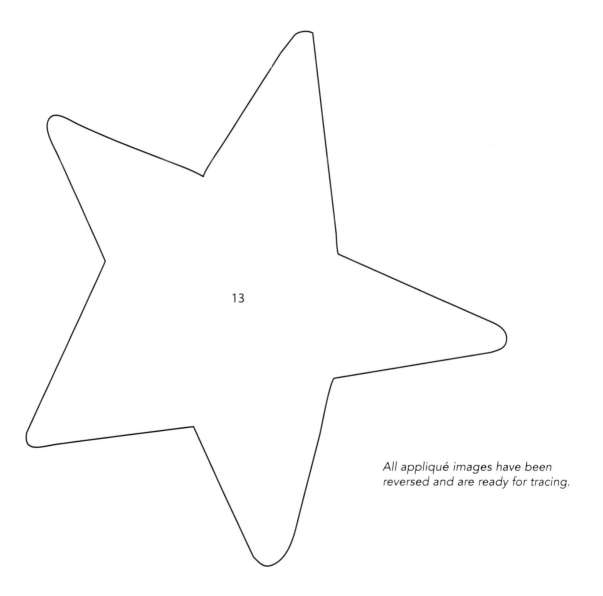

13

*All appliqué images have been
reversed and are ready for tracing.*

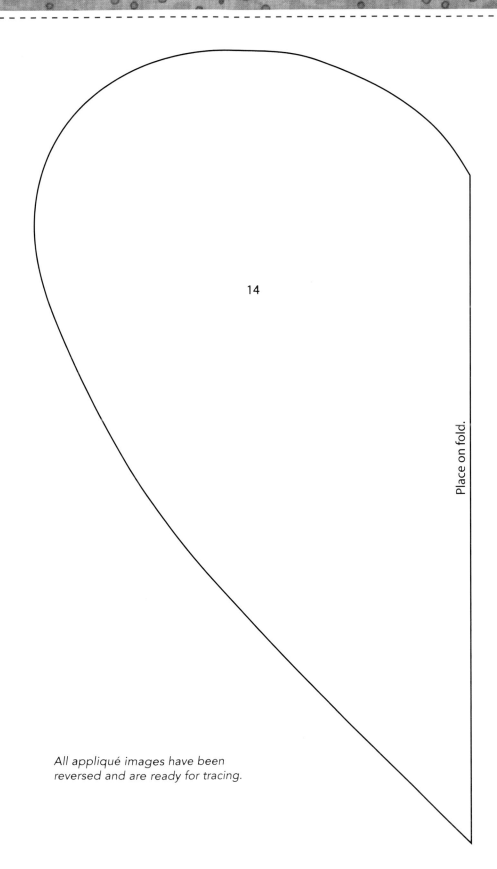

14

Place on fold.

*All appliqué images have been
reversed and are ready for tracing.*

Resources

Embellishments

FELT BALLS
Handbehg Felts
HandBEHGFelts.etsy.com

Crafty Wool Felt
craftywoolfelt.etsy.com

TaDaa Studio Felt
tadaastudiofelt.etsy.com

MILLINERY BIRDS
Kooky Krafts
kookykrafts.etsy.com

Craft Cabaret
craftcabaret.etsy.com

MILLINERY FLOWERS
Mary Not Martha
marynotmartha.etsy.com

PINCUSHION BOWLS, CERAMIC BUTTONS, RING BLANKS
Jennifer Jangles
jenniferjangles.com

POM-POM AND YO-YO MAKERS
Clover
clover-usa.com
Ask your favorite retailer.

PURSE HANDLES
Handmade Only
handmadeonly.etsy.com

Purse Making Supply
pursemakingsupply.etsy.com

SARI RIBBONS
Flea's Fibers
fleasfibers.etsy.com

UNIQUE TRIMS
Trimko
trimko.etsy.com

Little Red Cottage
littleredcottage.etsy.com

VINTAGE BUTTONS
Add Vintage
addvintage.etsy.com

Just Button Me
justbuttonme.etsy.com

VINTAGE FINDS
Chocolate Letters
chocolateletters.etsy.com

Fabric

COTTON FABRICS
In the Beginning Fabrics
inthebeginningfabrics.com
Ask your favorite
quilt shop.

DYEABLE VELVET AND VELVETEEN
Dharma Trading Co.
dharmatrading.com

DYED WOOL
Weeks Dye Works
weeksdyeworks.com

HAND-DYED VELVET
Blackberry Primitives
blackberryprimitives.com

PRINTED FELT
A Market Collection
amarketcollection.etsy.com

WOOL FELT
National Nonwovens
nationalnonwovens.com
(Wholesale only—ask your
favorite retailer.)

About the Author

It all started when Jennifer was four years old and received a Sew Perfect toy sewing machine. Her grandmother gave her a stack of upholstery fabric samples, and she jumped right into sewing. In high school her first job was at a fabric store, so she could basically spend her paycheck on more fabric. By high school, she had decided she wanted to run off to New York City and become a fashion designer. However, with an opening in her schedule for another art class, she took and fell in love with ceramics. She received her BFA in ceramics from Indiana University in 1995. She has been a self-supporting artist for 18 years, selling her ceramic tiles, beads, and jewelry.

In the back of her mind, Jennifer had always said she would go back to school to get her master's degree in textiles when she turned 36. Why 36? It just sounded like a good number; no reason at all. She was about to turn 36 and was considering her options for school, classes, and so on and then decided she wanted to design fabric more than anything. She taught herself, in her free time, and decided to see where that would take her.

Photo by Peter M. Frey

After a year of consistently working on her port-folio, she headed to Quilt Market for a handful of meetings with fabric companies and a stomach full of nerves and excitement. Jennifer signed a contract with In the Beginning Fabrics right after the show and con-tinues to work with them. Currently she is designing her twelfth line of fabric for them. Alongside designing fabric, Jennifer has a line of sewing patterns and craft kits under the Jennifer Jangles name.